I0114989

Tea, Please

HERBAL TEA RECIPES FOR KIDS

To my kids.
Thanks for having tea with me.

INNATE INK
PUBLISHING

Innate Ink Publishing

Copyright © 2022 Iva Hart

ISBN 978-1-956668-13-1

All rights reserved.

Art by Finedigitalarts on Etsy
https://www.etsy.com/shop/Finedigitalarts
Commercial License purchased August 2022

Tea, Please

HERBAL TEA RECIPES FOR KIDS

IVA HART

Welcome

Dear Friend,

Welcome to Tea, Please! A book of herbal tea blends for kids.

Whether you're new to the delight of tea time or enjoy it regularly, I hope you'll find a treasure in this book.

I set out to create something the world didn't have yet. I searched high and low for a tea blend recipe book that would appeal to children's' tastes, and when I didn't find one, I decided to create one!

Making tea together is a great way to teach kids about the five senses (see, taste, touch, smell, hear) and opposites (hot and cold), and explore nature by learning about plants and where our food comes from.

It's my hope that this book will bring joy and learning to your home, and that tea time will be a time of connection filled with happy memories. Remember to take pictures, and be creative!

Iva ♡

Contents

Things You'll Need

The things you need to make tea are simple to find, and most households will have everything on hand (except maybe the ingredients).

- Something to drink from - Ceramic mugs, teacups, and thermoses are all great.

- Something to heat water in - tea kettle, stovetop pot, or glass measuring cup (anything microwave or stovetop safe).

- Something to hold and strain your tea blend - tea balls, small, fine mesh strainers, or disposable bags are fantastic options.

- Spoons - metal or wooden because it's not great to use plastic in hot water.

- Heat source - check out the "Heat" page for ideas.

- Sweetener of choice (see "Make it Sweet" on page X).

Milk of choice (see "Make it Creamy" on page X).

Tea blend of choice made with a recipe in this book.

Ingredients

I've tried to keep the ingredients in these tea blends very simple to find or grow. Many of the plants included grow in most climates. You could start your own tea garden! Clover might already grow in your yard or in a park near you. Always wash plants you forage.

Always be 100% certain of what you're picking before you eat or drink it! All clovers are edible, for instance, but other plants may have sneaky look-alikes that could make you sick.

Also, if you're pregnant or have certain health conditions you might need to avoid certain herbs. All of the herbs in this book are safe for most kids and adults, but please always do your own research.

If you don't have space or time for a garden and can't find the plants growing nearby, buy from a local grocery store, herbalist, or other supplier before going online. Your herbs will be fresher and it's best to shop local!

Buying online is also a great option.
Visit www.ivahartbooks.weebly.com for a list of sellers I recommend for the best freshness and quality, or research your own!

Three Steps

Making tea is simple. It just takes three easy steps! Older kids and teenagers can be taught how to safely make tea on their own. Younger children can participate with a grownup.

Follow these three steps, described in detail on the following pages.

Heat

Steep

Stir

Heat

You'll need a heat-safe container such as a microwave-safe mug, teapot, pot or electric kettle

Next, you'll need a heat source like wood- burning fire, microwave, stove, electric kettle or electric stove.

**KIDS HEAT WARNING :
Make sure a grown up is nearby to help, and unless you have permission from a grownup, don't make tea alone!**

While heating the water, put your tea blend in a tea ball, strainer, or bag to avoid drinking the leaves later.

Once your water is hot, it's time for the next step: **STEEP**!

Steep

Possibly the hardest part about making tea is the waiting. It only takes a few minutes, but when you're looking forward to a tasty, cozy drink, a few minutes can stretch on forever.

With herbal tea letting the herbs sit in the water to extract the flavor and benefits is called steeping.

Different teas need different lengths of steeping time to bring out their best. Steeping for too little time leads to watery, less flavorful teas. Likewise, steeping too long can make tea taste bitter and strong, even spicy, depending on the flowers, fruits, and spices used.

Each of the recipes has a recommended steep time based on my experience and personal taste. Feel free to adjust to your liking!

Fun tip: Clean up, make a treat, sing a song, or play a short game while waiting for your tea to steep and cool. Remember to set a timer to remove your tea ball or bag so it doesn't steep too long, and another so your tea doesn't get too cold!

Time to strain your tea and **STIR**!

Stir

After your tea steeps, there are a few more things that need to happen before you can drink.

First, you'll want your tea to cool so it doesn't burn your tongue. You can choose to wait and stir for several minutes, add milk, or make your tea iced.

A single ice cube can be used to cool tea for impatient littles, or you can teach them this song while they wait!

Polly Put the Kettle On

Polly put the kettle on,
Polly put the kettle on,
Polly put the kettle on,
We'll all have tea.

Sukey take it off again,
Sukey take it off again,
Sukey take it off again,
They've all gone away.

Make it Sweet

Most people, especially kids, won't take their tea straight or unsweetened. Tea is meant to be a pleasure enjoyed, not endured!

So sweeten to taste, just don't drown out the unique flavors with too much sugar. The right sweet addition will bring your cup of tea to life.

- *White sugar*
- *Turbinado sugar*
- *Honey*
- *Honey powder*
- *Agave*
- *Maple syrup*
- *Stevia*
- *Monkfruit*
- *Xylitol*
- *Flavored syrups (homemade flower and fruit syrups are especially nice!)*
- *Coffee creamer*
- *Simple syrup*

When making iced tea, add granular sweeteners or honey and stir to dissolve BEFORE adding ice. Otherwise, the sweetener won't blend well.

Let your kids to experiment with different amounts and types in different cups and taste test. Write down the results in the Notes section at the end of this book. It's a science experiment!

If you're using a liquid sweetener, get a bottle with a pump to dispense it or use a spoon for thicker sweeteners like honey.
Sugar cubes and packets are also a handy way to measure serving sizes.

NOTE: HONEY IS NEVER APPROPRIATE FOR CHILDREN UNDER THE AGE OF 1 YEAR, DUE TO THE RISK OF INFANT BOTULISM.

Make it Creamy

If you want your tea to have a smooth, creamy, milky flavor, try adding milk!

When milk is added to tea in larger amounts, or if you steep your tea in milk instead of water, this is considered a "tea latte," and it's so good!

Milk can cool tea for little tongues and mellow out stronger flavors for picky palates. There are so many options these days whether you drink regular dairy or not. Try any of the following:

- Cow milk
- Goat milk
- Cream
- Half n' half
- Almond milk
- Oat milk
- Coconut milk (canned or boxed)
- Rice milk
- Hemp milk
- Cashew milk
- Coffee creamer

Just remember, if you added lemon to your tea, fresh or otherwise, it will curdle the milk and make unpleasant floaty bits. Any acidic tea will curdle milk. Even most non-dairy milks! The taste is unlikely to be affected, and it's still safe to drink, it just won't look quite right.

In this book there are three recipes we don't recommend adding milk to. They are: Hibiscus Berry, Lemon Honey, and Lavender Blue (if you add lemon to watch it change colors).

Make it Cold

Craving a cool drink? Iced teas are a great-tasting healthy substitute for the more sugary and artificially flavored drinks usually served to kids.

You can make any tea iced! Just follow these simple directions:

- Make tea as usual. Let it steep for the recommended time.

- Add granulated or thick liquid sweeteners like honey while tea is still warm. Stir to dissolve.

- Fill a mug, tumbler, thermos, or pitcher with ice. Pile the ice on top until it's slightly taller than the cup!

- Add any flavorings or milk to the ice-filled cup.

- Pour the steeped tea over the top until the cup is full.

Fun tip: Freeze sweetened herbal teas in popsicle molds for iced tea pops! Add mint leaves or cut fruit for extra enjoyment.

The tea will be cool enough to drink right away! If you want it ice cold, wait a few minutes. Enjoy your sweet, cold drinks!

Tea Blend Recipes

Peppermint

Let's start out with one of the most basic and beloved infusions of all time - mint tea.

With only one ingredient, consider this blend as a foundation for loads of experimentation! You can add mint to pretty much any tea blend and it will taste great. Cooling, invigorating, and classic.

Try a different type of mint plant such as: spearmint, orange mint, lemon mint, chocolate mint, e.t.c. for a new experience!

INGREDIENTS:

1 TBSP Dried Mint

Add 1 TBSP dried mint leaves to 1 cup boiling water. Let steep. Longer steeping time will give a stronger, sometimes almost bitter flavor. Using fresh mint will change the flavor and amount needed.

Tip: use to energize the mind and cool the body. A perfect summer drink when made with ice!

Lemon honey tea is a classic combination for when one is sick, especially with a cold that comes with a cough or sore throat. The honey is soothing and the heat is relaxing. The lemon helps clean out the body's gunk.

INGREDIENTS:

1 TBSP Fresh Lemon Juice (about half of a lemon, squeezed)

1 TBSP Honey (or more to taste)

Heat water. If using fresh lemon, separate the juice from the seeds. If you can't get fresh lemon juice, you can use concentrate from a bottle, but you may need to use less due to its stronger flavor and acidity.

Add honey while tea is still hot, to your preferred tastes. Honey is better than sugar in this tea if you're sick, due to its antimicrobial and soothing properties.

Lemon Honey

STEEP TIME: 2 MINUTES

Tip: If drinking when sick, add a pinch of cinnamon or ginger for an extra boost of healing goodness.

Lavender Blue

Magic is everywhere - even in your cup of tea! This tea turns out a beautiful blue color. And if you add a squeeze of lemon, your tea will magically change. Give it a try!

INGREDIENTS:

6 Tablespoons Butterfly Pea Flowers

3 Tablespoons Lavender Flowers

Mix herbs together in a jar or container. Crush or blend Butterfly Pea Flowers beforehand to create a more consistent blend.

Use 1 Tablespoon of Lavender Blue tea blend in 1 cup boiling water for a single serving.

Tip: Lavender is famous for it's sleep-inducing qualities. Brew a cup right before bedtime for sweet dreams!

Chamomile flowers are white with yellow centers, like tiny daisies. When brewed, they taste light and floral with a hint of natural sweetness, and might make you feel calm or even drowsy! Lemon balm is a tasty, mood-lifting addition.

INGREDIENTS:

3 TBSP Dried Chamomile Flowers

3 TBSP Dried Lemon Balm

Add 1 TBSP combined leaves to 1 cup water. Follow steeping directions. This tea is especially good with a splash of your favorite milk!

Chamomile Calm

STEEP TIME: 3 MINUTES

Tip: use when you need to calm anxious feelings or have a hard time falling asleep.

Hibiscus Berry

Hibiscus flowers and blueberries create a gorgeous, bright red tea. It's fruity and mood-lifting, and the color makes it really fun to drink!

INGREDIENTS:

4 TBSP Dried Hibiscus Flowers

3 TBSP Freeze-dried Blueberries (dehydrated may work)

1/2 tsp Cinnamon stick pieces (or 1 stick, or 1/4 tsp ground cinnamon)

Use a food processor, blender, or mortar and pestle to break up the fruit and flowers before adding the cinnamon. Add 1 TBSP to 1 cup hot water. Follow steeping time and enjoy!

**Hibiscus is an acidic flower. Don't add milk or it will curdle!

Tip: This tea is good for when you feel "stuck" emotionally. Also, the antioxidants give an amazing boost to your immune system!

23

This super-nutrient, golden tea is so calming for an upset stomach! Add peppercorns to activate the pain-relieving qualities of the turmeric and give your tea a subtle, spicy kick. Kids may or may not tolerate peppercorns in their tea, so adjust quantity according to their taste!

INGREDIENTS:

1 TBSP Dried Ginger Root

2 TBSP Dried Turmeric Root

Black Peppercorns (a few - optional)

Mix ingredients together and add 1 teaspoon to a tea ball, tea bag, or strainer in 1 cup of hot water. Let steep 3-5 minutes. For a stronger tea, steep longer.

Ginger Turmeric

STEEP TIME: 3-5 MINUTES

Tip: drink this tea to relieve pain and inflammation, upset stomach, and symptoms of cold and flu.

Warm Spice

This warming tea is especially good on cold days. It's more flavorful than hot chocolate and the spices even help your body fight colds! Your cup of tea will smell like the holidays and bring warmth to you body and your heart with each sip.

INGREDIENTS:

1 tsp Cinnamon stick pieces

1 tsp Cardamom pods (crushed)

1 pinch Ground or shaved nutmeg

1 tsp Ginger root

1/2 tsp Whole Cloves

2 TBSP Red Rooibos loose leaf

Add 1 TBSP of herbs to 1 cup boiling water and steep.

Tip: This tea recipe is loosely based on the popular Chai recipes. Chai goes extra good with holiday cookies or after playing in the snow!

25

Suprisingly high in vitamins and minerals, all clover flowers are edible and make great teas! Forage these blossoms in your yard or public park. Be sure to wash and dry completely before using for tea!

INGREDIENTS:

3 TBSP Dried Clover Flowers, any variety

1 TBSP Dried Orange Peels

Add 1 TBSP of tea blend to 1 cup boiling water. Steep 4 minutes and enjoy warm or iced.

What would it taste like with dried vanilla bean instead of orange peels? Try adding lemon peels, lemon juice, mint leaves, or dried fruit for fun twists!

Sweet Clover

**STEEP TIME:
4 MINUTES**

Tip: this tea is energizing and encourages a positive attitude. Orange peels also ward off sickness.

Make Your Own Tea Blends

Now you're ready to try your hand at making your own unique tea blends!

Start by making small changes to the recipes in this book. Maybe you like more cinnamon. Maybe you want to try raspberry or peach instead of blueberry. Maybe you want to combine mint with another flavor (mint goes with lots of things!)

Whatever you try next, you're going to want to write down the recipes and the results, just like a real scientist.

That's why we've provided a few pages in the back of this book especially for your notes.

The possibili-TEAS are endless!

Find us Online

Scan the QR code or visit the website below for bonus recipes, a list of items to buy from Amazon, and other online sources!

SCAN ME

www.ivahartbooks.weebly.com

Send us Your Pictures!

Make tea together and send your pictures to
ivahartbooks@gmail.com

You'll be featured on the author's instagram, tiktok, or website to
show others the joy of making tea together!

About the Author

Iva Hart is a published author and homeschooling mother to six kids. She lives in Iowa with her family and two cats.

Iva has a passion for learning about edible plants and urban foraging. She wanted to share her knowledge and love of edible plants in a way that enabled families to spend more positive, quality time learning and laughing together, and so this book was born.

Curling up with a good book and a cup of tea is one of her favorite past times.

We hope it's your favorite now, too!

Notes

Notes

_____

_____

_____

_____

_____

_____

_____

_____

_____

_____

Notes

_____

_____

_____

_____

_____

_____

_____

_____

_____

_____

Notes

_____

_____

_____

_____

_____

_____

_____

_____

_____

_____

www.ingramcontent.com/pod-product-compliance
Lightning Source LLC
Chambersburg PA
CBHW041547260326
41914CB00016B/1569